Effigy of Horatio Lord Nelson now in the Westminster Abbey Museum.

(Reproduced by kind permission of the Dean and Chapter of Westminster.)

2

HORATIO, ADMIRAL LORD NELSON

Was he . . . a Mason?

Written and researched by
John Webb

First published in England in 1998
by Ian Allan/Lewis Masonic
Riverdene Business Park, Molesey Road,
Hersham, Surrey KT12 4RG
who are members of the Ian Allan Group.

ISBN 85318218 3

Printed and bound in Great Britain
by Ian Allan Printing Ltd,
Riverdene Business Park,
Molesey Road, Hersham,
Surrey KT12 4RG
Tel: 01932 266600

ABOUT THE AUTHOR

JOHN WEBB K.St.J.J.P.P.G St.B., is Secretary and Past Master of Quatuor Coronati Lodge No.2076. Born on 26 March 1918 at Finchley in North London, he was educated at Christ's College and on leaving school he joined the Royal Regiment of Artillery in 1936. After a Staff College Course he was commissioned and became an Instructor of Gunnery in England, India and Burma. At the end of the war he left the Regiment in 1946 to attend at London University where he studied Anatomy, Physiology and Physiotherapy. Appointed Superintendent Physiotherapist to the Whittington Hospital, he started the first clinic for the treatment of injured athletes and sports persons. Offered the opportunity of doing research by Philips Electrical Ltd in respect of electro-medical equipment, he became a Commercial Executive with the Dutch firm before joining the Most Venerable Order of the Hospital of St. John of Jerusalem as Director of Supplies for the St. John Ambulance Association and Brigade, and the Ophthalmic Hospital in Jerusalem. On his retirement in 1983, he was honoured by H.M. The Queen by being appointed a Knight of the Most Venerable Order of St. John.

A keen sportsman, particularly in the water, he has represented England as a springboard diver and in 1947 he participated in, and won, the Springboard Diving Championship of England. As well as competing for many years he was a sports commentator for the B.B.C. and wrote on sport for the *Guardian, Observer* and the *Daily Mirror*.

John Webb became a Freemason in 1943 whilst serving with the Army in Karachi where he joined Lodge Scinde 4284. Transferred to Tatanagar in 1944, he joined Lodge Tisco 3865 where he was passed and raised and joined the Royal Arch Chapter. Returning to England at the end of hostilities he joined the Old Finchleians Lodge No.5409. He is a founder member of the Prior Walter Lodge 8687 formed by members of the St. John Ambulance and from the Order and was its Master in 1980. A joining member of the Lodge of Friendship No.6. he was honoured by being chosen as Master in 1984 and nominated to be the Grand Steward the following year. His activities have not been restricted to the Craft for he is an active member of the Royal Arch, Knights Templar, Ancient and Accepted Rite, and Societas Rosicrucian in Anglia.

His first paper to the Quatuor Coronati Lodge was entitled 'The Order of St. John and the connection with Freemasonry'. He was invited to become a full Member of the Lodge in 1981 and delivered a further paper 'Josef Haydn, Freemason and Musician'. He has always been ready to make comment on papers presented to the Lodge. In 1995, he was honoured by being appointed as the Prestonian Lecturer choosing the subject of 'Freemasonry and Sport'. He is well known as a lecturer to Lodges throughout the country and abroad and talks on many subjects including 'Rudyard Kipling', 'Robert Burns', 'The last year of Mozart', 'The Gentleman's Magazine' and others.

FREEMASONS' HALL,

GREAT QUEEN STREET,

LONDON, WC2B 5AZ

9 February 1998

John Webb is an enthusiast who is also a Freemason, and he has turned his attention to a question which will interest many Freemasons.

His account of Lord Nelson's life will disappoint some, who might have hoped for further light on their hero as a thoughtful and daring tactician at a time when the Fighting Instructions discouraged innovation, a fine seaman even in those days of high seamanship, and an inspiring leader of men.

John Webb does, however, lay ample emphasis on Nelson's high sense of vocation and duty. It might have been too much if he had been able to show that Nelson was a Freemason: many would think that the traditions of the Navy were enough to mould or confirm Nelson's approach to his service. Thinking Freemasons would, I hope, be generous about this - if Nelson had been a Mason, his membership of their Craft would have been a happy accident in the life of a man who already possessed the qualities they look for.

John is perhaps too diffident in his final verdict. Mariners will recognise that the brotherhood of the sea is a kind of Freemasonry - a whole series of common experiences giving rise to or explaining a code of conduct, which Masons might call morality. In this sense, Freemasons would be proud to agree that Nelson was, in *almost* every particular, their Brother.

MBS HIGHAM
Commander, Royal Navy,
Grand Secretary

6

FOREWORD

By W.Bro. Captain P.J. Bootherstone, DSC, RN

Many regard Admiral Lord Nelson as the first truly national hero of our Country. Certainly, the news of his death caused widespread sadness at the time and today, nearly 200 years later, his memory is still revered. Every year in the village of Madron near Penzance, there is held a Royal Navy parade followed by a church service to commemorate Nelson's death, as it was here that the news of his death first reached the British Isles. Countless books have attempted to explain why it should be that a one armed, one eyed sailor of indifferent health should be so revered. Quite rightly they mention his charisma and brilliance as a leader who could inspire loyalty and devotion in his men and they comment on his outstanding personal qualities. This well researched book by W.Bro. John Webb highlights some very interesting and less well known facets of his life which further add to our knowledge of a truly remarkable man and I warmly commend it to you.

GENESIS OR THE REASON WHY?

So often, as one is going round to different Lodges, I am asked about the research which is done by Members of the Quatuor Coronati Lodge No. 2076. It is a Lodge which was founded over 100 years ago by a group of Brethren who were interested in research into many of the problems connected with the start and continuance of Freemasonry. They were interested in Truth, History, and above all extending the knowledge they gained by investigating the Genesis of Freemasonry. They did not have available to them in those very early days Computers, or even Electric and Manual typewriters. They had a grim doggedness which kept the candles burning far into the night, and they had an ambition to succeed and publish the results of their studies to a wider group than those who had the exclusive membership of the Quatuor Coronati Lodge to help and guide them.

For myself, I was fortunate to be invited to give a lecture on 'Sport and Freemasonry' to the Portsmouth and District Installed Masters Lodge by W.Bro.Cdr. Hardy. Following the Lecture we dined and then I went to the home of Cdr. Hardy who had invited me to spend the night there and return to London in the morning.

In the company of my Host and his charming wife I could not fail to have a wonderful evening. The 'Islay' whiskey came out and I learned that Arthur Hardy was at one time, not only connected with the Navy for most of his life, he was also O/C of the Portsmouth Dockyards and had a detailed and intimate knowledge of the 'Victory'.

I was shown details of this great Vessel and many other things were explained to me that I began to wonder if the life of Admiral Lord Nelson had ever been written up and if he had any connection with Freemasonry. I decided to start the ball rolling, and to find out all that I could about this small but intense man.

I started by going to the British Library and looking at the list of books which had been written about Horatio Nelson. It was immense, and I could not visualise reading every one. I made a list of those that I had been advised to read, and started on the long journey. At the British Library also, in the Document Section, I saw on exhibition the last letter that Nelson wrote to Lady Hamilton. I was handed a book of letters that conveyed the intensity of feelings which he had not only for Lady Hamilton, but for all of his family, especially his father.

It was then that I started to type the result of my researches. It was then, also, that I made a journey to the Norfolk Installed Masters Lodge in Norwich. Here, my host was W.Bro.Peter Racey, and he and his charming wife made me feel very much at home, the more especially when I learned that Peter had written a Play about Nelson some time earlier. The world indeed is a small place, I felt compelled to sit down and write the 'Story of Nelson'. I had to ask myself the question posed on the front and introduction of this small book:

WAS HORATIO, LORD NELSON, A FREEMASON?

SEEK AND YE SHALL FIND.

NELSON'S RANKS

29 September	1758 Born	
ac.1 January 1771	Midshipman	Aged 12
24 September 1776	Acting Lieutenant	Aged 17
9 April 1777	Lieutenant	Aged 18
8 December 1778	Commander	Aged 20
11 June 1779	Captain	Aged 20
4 April 1796	Acting Commodore: second class	Aged 37
11 August 1796	Commodore: first class	Aged 37
20 February 1797	Rear-Admiral of the Blue	Aged 38
17 May 1797	Knight of the Bath	Aged 38
6 November 1798	Peer of the Realm	Aged 40
14 February 1799	Rear-Admiral of the Red	Aged 40
13 August 1799	Duke of Brontë, Sicily	Aged 40
1 January 1801	Vice-Admiral of the Blue	Aged 42
22 May 1801	Viscount	Aged 42
23 April 1804	Vice-Admiral of the White	Aged 45
	– Nelson died in this rank, 1805	Aged 47

HORATIO, LORD NELSON, WAS HE A MASON?

On 29th September 1758, a son was born to Edmund and Catherine Nelson in the house allocated to the rector of the small village of Burnham Thorpe which is in Norfolk. He was not the only child born into this family and when in 1767, Mrs Nelson died she left eight of eleven children in the care of her husband. Mrs Nelson was directly related to Sir Robert Walpole, her maiden name being Suckling. The name chosen for this new child was very much in keeping with family wishes and was that of his godfather the second Lord Walpole.

The death of the mother, when Horatio was but nine years of age, obviously put a considerable strain on the father, and it must have been with some welcome relief that the brother of the late mother visited the home and became known to the boys, and more especially to Horatio. It could not have come as a surprise therefore, when some three years later, the young Horatio expressed a wish to be able to join his uncle (who was a Captain in the Navy) in his profession. Captain Suckling was written to, and despite reservations concerning the young man's health and strength, he arranged for him to join a ship called 'Raisonnable', which was at that time in the Medway near to Chatham. Escorted by his father to London, he was then put on the Chatham Stage and set down at the nearest point to the ship and then left to find his own way aboard. Miserable, lonely and feeling lost, it was possibly fortunate for the young man that he met an officer who happened to know his uncle and who was able to direct his steps in the right direction to the ship. On mounting the gang plank to reach the deck of the vessel, he learned that his uncle was not there, and was not expected back for several days. The boy was entirely lost and bewildered. Eventually he was directed to make his way down two steep sets of steps into the bowels of the ship and there to put his baggage. With assistance from one of the crew, he fixed his hammock with those of the other midshipmen.

Thus he started on his life as a member of His Majesty's Navy. Cold, desolate, lonely and apparently forgotten.

What sort of boy was Horatio at this age? We know from written accounts of stories of the family that the three sons, Maurice, William and Horatio were very different in physical build, and in nature. Maurice was marked out by his uncle as not being the type of material of which Navy Officers were made. His brothers were of a different class. William was a big lad and had the reputation of being a 'bully'. The story is told by the sister of an occasion when William and Horatio were fighting together, and she was asked to intervene and separate them because 'William was so much bigger and stronger', she replied by saying "Leave them alone, because Horace will beat him!". Horatio was audacious, lively and fearless, with a great sense of determination, and above all a will to succeed.

When Captain Suckling returned to his command, he lost no time in summoning his new Midshipman to his cabin. He there took the opportunity of explaining the complexities of life in the Royal Navy. A midshipman was not a commissioned officer. That was a step which would be gained with the passing of the examinations for advancement to the rank of Lieutenant. In the meantime he had plenty of work to do in absorbing the discipline and learning the required seamanship. The great vessel was being prepared for action and after days of helping to load the store rooms with food, three further days were spent in assisting in the heavy work of loading the guns. There would be the twenty-six heavy guns which would be mounted on the lower gun-deck on either side, to be followed with a like number of eighteen pounders to be sited on the decks above.

There was another side to the life in the Navy as practised in the Medway, and it was in these first weeks that the young Nelson was brought face to face with the realities of discipline and punishment. The whole ship's company were assembled on an upper deck to witness punishment. Twice he was witness to a sailor being tied to a grating and flogged with a cat-o'-nine tails wielded by a boatswain's mate. In this way they dealt with the crimes of theft, drunkenness and brawling. It was part of the 'hardening' process for the young twelve-year-old, but the time had come for the ship to be moved down the Medway. The expectation of service in an active role gave the real meaning to the tightness of the discipline in binding together the crew as a team equipped to fight the enemy in extreme conditions.

Life for Horatio Nelson was not to continue on board the 'Raisonable' mainly for two reasons. The first, was that the ship had been moved down the Medway to a little dockyard where the fitting for 'Active' service was to continue. This did not happen, for the threat of war lessened. The urgent need for the warship was dispensed with and the Admiralty took time to consider whether or not to return her to the reserve list. The second reason lay in the fact that Captain Suckling was given command of another bigger ship named the 'Triumph' which proudly carried seventy-four guns. This great warship was a 'guard' vessel and was mainly concerned with the security at the mouth of the Thames and Medway.

Nelson did not join his uncle on the new command, but he did help to row him across the intervening waters together with his possessions. Captain Suckling must have given the young lad his very serious consideration. He arranged for a friend of his to take Horatio as a member of his crew on a ship soon to sail to the Caribbean. The idea was formed with good common sense. His new Captain was John Rathbone, at one time a former officer with Captain Suckling, and now only too pleased to have the young nephew of his good friend aboard. There is no doubt that Nelson would learn more about the art of seamanship on the long journey across to the other side of the Atlantic than being on a Guardship in the Thames. Now for the first time he experienced the swell of the waves, the freshness of the salty air, the chill of sickness caused by the wind and the waves, and the development of the team spirit as men worked together in a unity of respect and kindness. He later wrote home to say "I returned a practical seaman", and with that he quoted "Aft the more honour, forward the better man!".

A year later he returned to the 'Triumph' and his uncle remarked on the new confidence he had gained after his voyages across the Atlantic.. Horatio himself remarked, "It was many weeks before I got in the least reconciled to a man of war". The boy was changing and becoming a man and now he was to be given the opportunity by his uncle of experiencing his first command. Already, he had taken charge of small ship's boats, now he was given a small, but prize job, of being in charge of the warship's cutter. It was an honour usually reserved for the midshipman who had done well in the studies relative to navigation. His command required the knowledge of the Medway and the Thames, and with pride and confidence he sailed the river past the Royal Hospital at Greenwich, the dockyards at Woolwich and the Pool of London even to the Tower of London and St. Paul's Cathedral. Later he wrote, "I became a good pilot for vessels of that description".

Nelson's return to the care of his uncle in the guardship, however, had alerted his guardian to another fact, namely that his stay on the merchant ship had soured his taste for life in the Navy. The appointment to take charge of the cutter enabled him to learn much about the Thames and the many fine Navy ships lying on the waters.

THE ARCTIC ADVENTURE

His enthusiasm was rekindled when he learned that two fine vessels were being equipped to make a trip to the North Pole and Arctic regions. His uncle reminded him that a strict attention to his navigational studies could result in his being recommended for service on one of the vessels being fitted. So it worked out, and indeed he was recommended by Captain Suckling to the second in command of the expedition, to be admitted as coxswain to Captain Lutwidge.

The two vessels chosen to be re-fitted were coastal bombardment ships and were undoubtedly very strong. Nevertheless, additional strengthening took place and then 'Racehorse' and 'Carcass' were declared ready to depart. This they did on 4th June 1773 on an expedition backed by the Royal

Society and commanded by a young man of under thirty years of age named Captain the Honourable Constantine Phipps. The young Horatio had transferred his baggage to the 'Carcass' and found much to interest him in new equipment and fellow travellers. He realised that this voyage was to be much more than a survey to determine a Northern passage. There were scientists aboard who would be 'trying out' new methods of navigation and speed measurement. Apart from his own duties, there was much to interest a boy who, as yet, had not reached sixteen years of age.

The many books written about Nelson and his Arctic adventures contain no better story other than that told by Captain Lutwidge. From this good friend we are told of an adventure when one night, Nelson with another companion made their way from the vessel and across to the solid ice which surrounded both warships. Their object was to try and secure a bear skin. It was not long before their absence was noted and the two hunters were observed some distance from the ship in process of attacking a large bear. The signal was made for their return and Nelson's friend urged him to obey it.

Nelson at this point was separated from the bear by a rather large chasm, on the other hand, he had no ammunition and would have found difficulty in dealing with such a fierce animal. His companion had returned to the ship, but Nelson seemed determined to carry on with the fight to get the bear. The Captain ordered a blank charge to be fired from the gun which caused the bear to be scared off. Nelson returned to the ship where he was questioned about his motive for wanting to kill a bear. The young midshipman answered, "Captain, Sir, I wished to kill the bear and carry the skin back for my father". His courage, endurance and fortitude were to be tested thoroughly in the course of this Arctic Expedition. He would return incredibly more mature than his years would suggest.On the return the crew of the 'Carcass' were paid off, and Nelson, not yet fifteen years old was transferred as a midshipman to the warship 'Seahorse' in which he was to serve two years.

FAITH AND DUTY

The experience he had gained in sailing first, with a merchant ship to the West Indies, and then with the Navy to the Arctic taught him the basic principles of 'Sea Lore'. He had learned about the winds, the weather and the tides. The sailors on the merchantman had ensured that he learned about the ropes and the rigging, together with the setting of sails . As a parson's son he must have stood on occasions to watch the waves and then to study the clear but starlit sky overhead. In these contemplative moments he worked out for himself the meaning of the word 'Duty'. It became part of his in-born religion. Simple and yet definite, faith in the God proscribed for the family by a devout father. He had an awareness brought about by his proximity to the sea and the stars. It was a faith which would stay with him until the moment of his death.

Before he was eighteen, he had sailed to the East Indies, and like so many at that time he became very ill with Malaria. Recovering from this but not cured, he fell victim to two other common illnesses, dysentery and then scurvy. Death was at times not far distant from him, and when during the voyage, the 'Seahorse' called in at Bombay at the end of the year 1775, he was so ill that he was not expected to live. Fortunately, he was examined by a surgeon sent to see him by the Admiral of the Fleet, who ordered Nelson to be sent home to England in a ship called the 'Dolphin'. The voyage home started on 23rd March 1775. The ship was comfortable and the sea calm for the first few days. The month of April, however, brought storms, lightning, and torrential rain. The weather could not have been worse. The ship was thrown about and many of the crew were injured. In this period the Boatswain died and the young Nelson was sick, sleepless and exhausted. He too nearly joined the list of casualties, but somehow, his faith kept him alive. He survived. The ship eventually docked in Simon's Bay in the shadow of Table Mountain, South Africa, two months after setting out. Here, the 'Dolphin' was forced to undergo an extensive re-fit and repairs were done on the torn sails and damaged decks. During this period in a warm, cool and nice climate, with soft breezes and plenty of fresh good food, the cure to the frail body was brought about. When they sailed again on 20th June, his health was much improved, but his strength had mostly gone. He was but a skeleton compared with the fit young man who had started out. At the end of this year he was invalided out from his ship with malaria, and given time to make a complete recovery. It was at this time that he spoke of his spiritual thoughts and his feelings.

"I felt impressed with a feeling that I should never rise in my profession. My mind was staggered with a view of the difficulties I had to surmount and the little interest I possessed, I could discover no means of reaching the object of my ambition."

It was at this stage, with his health returning, he experienced what he described as a visitation. "After a long and gloomy reverie, in which I wished myself overboard, a sudden glow of patriotism was kindled within me and presented my King and Country as my patron". "Well, then," I exclaimed, "I will be a hero and, confiding in Providence, I will brave every danger."

This feeling of peace and happiness as a motivating force within the young seaman must surely have been bred within him, and be directly related to his father, the devout parish priest. It was to characterise him in every station of life, and be directly responsible for the great love he generated amongst those who recognised him as a leader, with a great, and supreme quality of mercy.

PROMOTION

On 9th April 1777, he passed the examinations which earned him promotion to Lieutenant, and was immediately posted to the frigate 'Lowestoft' then being fitted out to undergo a voyage to the West Indies. He arrived at Port Royal, Jamaica on 19th July and within one year had gained promotion to be first lieutenant in the 'Bristol'. In England his uncle Captain Maurice Suckling died. He bequeathed to his nephew a small sum of money and exhorted him, "My boy, I leave you to my country; serve her well and she'll never desert but will ultimately reward you".

Captain Horatio Nelson painted by Jean Francis Rigaud (1742-1810).

Begun in 1777 when he was a Lieutenant but finished in 1781, for his friend and Commander Captain Locker. The background commemorates his part in the Don Juan River expedition.

(Reproduced by kind permission of the National Maritime Museum at Greenwich.)

These words sent to him by his dying Uncle, must have made a lasting impression in the young Lieutenant's mind. He was now twenty years of age, and in this year two further appointments were extended to him. He was appointed First-Lieutenant of the 'Bristol', and in the December of this year of 1778, he was given the appointment as Commander of the 'Badger'. In both appointments he did well and it was no surprise that in the June of the following year he was further promoted as Post-Captain of the 'Hinchinbroke'. In tracing these promotions, it is interesting to note that a very good friend of his, Cuthbert Collingwood, always succeeded Nelson when he moved on, and up in rank. In this year also Spain joined with France against Britain.

Nelson was most fortunate in possessing a lively interest in his profession at the time when it could be of great advantage to him. The promotions had been quite rapid and deserved, and as yet, he was just at his twenty-first year. He had demonstrated his ability as an officer. His letters, orders and official communications demonstrate a shrewd ability in dealing with those superior to himself in rank. He was well liked by his fellow officers, and thoroughly backed by the members of his crews. In 1780, the opportunity to distinguish himself in a campaign known as the San Juan Expedition, found him in the 'Hinchinbrook' conveying five hundred men from Port Royal to a destination in the Honduras. This particular campaign brought no great honour to Nelson. Historians now discount the effectiveness of the operation, which involved the siege and capture of the Castle San Juan. Many men were lost due to fevers and illness which did greater damage than the Spaniards. Eventually victory was achieved, but Nelson was so ill that he had to be removed back to Port Royal where he was carried ashore in his cot. Following his previous illness, he was now diagnosed as suffering from typhoid fever; at the same time he was appointed to take command of the 'Janus', a vessel of 44 guns. Nelson was too ill and he had to ask leave to return to England, he therefore gave up his command and was returned to England by his friend Captain (later Admiral) Cornwallis sailing in the 'Lion'. On arrival he went immediately to Bath where he underwent three months of care and attention before he made application for employment from their Lordships in the Admiralty. He was rewarded by being appointed to the 'Albemarle', a former French ship of some 28 guns.

The winter of this year he spent in sailing the North Sea in this very strange vessel. From time to time Nelson experienced the feeling that the vessel was going to turn over caused by the extreme lengths of the masts. Returning to England and the dockyard, he had the masts shortened before he received new orders to sail to Quebec. In accordance with his orders Nelson sailed for Canada and in one of his many sorties captured a fishing schooner. He treated the Captain of this vessel with great kindness and in return the master made a present to Nelson of quantities of fresh food in the form of meat, water and other provisions. Nelson in return gave the Captain a certificate exempting his vessel from being captured by any other vessel. It was a rare act of generosity, the certificate is preserved to this day in Boston. It was whilst he was at this station that he was attracted to a young lady. It was due to a good friend, Alexander Davidson, that Nelson did not proceed with a rather imprudent marriage. Davidson persuaded him that his life at that moment really belonged to his service in the Navy. It was possibly fortunate that upon reflection Nelson agreed with him, and he therefore rejoined his ship and sailed off to carry out the orders he had been given. In turn he was introduced by Lord Hood to the Duke of Clarence, Prince William Henry with whom he became quite friendly. The Prince was informed that Nelson was well versed in tactics. The two young men became firm friends from that moment.

The signing of a Peace agreement meant the recall of the 'Albermarle' to England where the crew were paid off. Nelson took the opportunity of visiting Bath, in which beautiful city he took full advantage of the medical facilities available to assist him in recovering from his severe illnesscs.

It must be stated that Nelson added to his personal character a very romantic nature. With an old shipmate Captain James Macnamara of the 'Bristol', he launched into a journey to France, which country was on the edge of revolution. His object was to learn to speak French. The two friends crossed to Calais and made their way to St. Omer. In this town they booked into a Lodging House run by a Madam La Mourie, whose two daughters did not speak English. "Therefore," said Nelson, "I must learn to speak French if 'tis only for the pleasure of speaking with them as they speak no English."

The French lessons did not proceed however, for there was also staying in the Lodging House an English Parson who had brought over to France with him his two very attractive daughters. This caused a letter to be written to his brother William saying, "My heart is quite secured against the French beauties: I almost wish that I could say as much for an English young lady". The affair did not proceed for he realised that he was in no position financially to offer marriage, and although he wrote home for help, it was not forthcoming and the romance ended sadly and gently. Such affairs happened quite often, but they terminated with gentlemanly courtesy and kindness and no harm done.

MARRIAGE

On 11th March 1787, Captain Nelson married Mrs Frances Nisbet, a widow. She was 27 years of age and a few months older that Nelson. Previously married to a Doctor who had died at Salisbury she had one son. She met Nelson when he visited the island of Nevis, and it was there at the house of Montpelier that the wedding took place. Prince William Henry escorted the bride, and an officer from the 'Boreal' acted as best man to the groom. "Until I married I never knew happiness." Thus quoted Nelson after the toast had been given to the happy couple by the Prince.

During the time that he was on this station, he paid great attention to the health and happiness of his crew. The ship was kept constantly on the move, and in periods of bad weather when the 'Boreal' took shelter in the English Harbour, he ensured that everyone was kept happy by entertainments, music and sporting matches. On his return to London he could report that the crew had suffered no losses or days lost due to illness.

The next few years in his life have been described by one writer as being the 'period of being on the Beach'. The Crew had been paid off from the 'Boreal' and Nelson was under the impression that he had been badly treated. He considered the possibility of retiring from the Navy, and would have done so, but for the good and generous advice given to him by Lord Hood, who induced him not to proceed with that thinking. However, he had not wasted his time for he had introduced his wife to his family and other relatives, and attended to many other domestic matters. One of these concerned giving evidence for, and on behalf of, a member of his crew accused of murder. His plea on behalf of the man was so detailed, and well prepared, that the court decided that the plea of 'Insanity' put forward by Nelson was justified, and the man's life was saved. The winter of 1792 saw an end to his frustrations and he was appointed to the command of the 'Agamemnon' a large vessel of 64 guns. On the 1 st February 1793, France formally declared war on Britain. It is recorded that on 7th February 1793, Captain Nelson trod the decks of his new command after a lapse of five years. His duty dictated that he should go to his cabin and there record in the Ship's Log, 'Fresh gales with wind at times. Went on board and put the ship in commission. Found the carpenter and joiner at work.' His frustrations were at an end, but his irritability can be remarked in letters written to Fanny. Before him lay the urge to get the vessel ready for adventure at sea.

The next period of years allowed Nelson to gain a much more detailed knowledge of the duties of a senior officer of the Navy. He was well liked by those who controlled the Admiralty, received invitations to the Royal levees, and more than that, he was engaged in many operations against the French whilst sailing in the Mediterranean.

The 'Agamemnon' was ordered to the Mediterranean where the Fleet was commanded by Lord Hood. It should be remembered that France, at this time, was in a state of horrific revolution. The Fleet arrived in the waters to the south of France at a strategic moment when the people in the south would willingly have separated from the north, and formed a separate French Republic As it was, Lord Hood negotiated with the people of Toulon, to take over their city and a very good port. It was realised that more men were needed to have any advantage, and to enforce security. Accordingly Nelson was sent on a diplomatic mission to Naples, where Sir William Hamilton was the British Ambassador and who would be able to use his Diplomatic status with the King of Naples to secure the support of a large number of Neapolitan troops. Against continuous attacks from the Jacobin French the town was defended from August to December 1793. It was at this time that Nelson made his first contact with Sir William and Lady Hamilton without realising that this would start the destruction of his own domestic happiness. He now took part in many skirmishes both at sea, and sometimes, on land. It was in one of these land assaults that he was wounded. A shot hit the ground near to where he was standing, gravel and sand were both thrown up with considerable force into his face causing considerable damage to his face and to one of his eyes. He did not think that the injury was serious but admitted he could only distinguish light and shade, and was not able to see clearly from that eye. In modern terms, it is probable that the retina of the eye was displaced, but there was nothing that could be done in those days.

The years between 1797 and 1799 brought a series of failures and successes. 1797 saw Nelson engaged in an expedition to Tenerife. Historians writing of this period, all seem to classify the action as a disaster. Certainly, from a personal point of view, Nelson did suffer the loss of an arm. The records show, "1797. July 25. Admiral Nelson . . . Compound fracture of the right arm by a musket ball passing through just above the elbow. An artery divided. The arm was amputated immediately and opium afterwards was given." It was arranged that Nelson should sail for home aboard the 'Seahorse' in company with another wounded Officer. He arrived home to be with his wife, father and one other relative on Sunday 3rd September. This suited him well for a short time. It was important, however, to return to London, where the best Medical attention was available to him to assist in the recovery from his wound and surgery. This period of enforced rest was to his benefit. In this period also, he was promoted to the rank of Rear Admiral, and was able also to attend an investiture at the Palace where he was thanked and congratulated by the King. On the 17th May 1797 he was created a K.B. He was able to attend to his financial matters, and was of course in receipt of a disability-ability payment of one thousand pounds per annum. His relationship with his wife was closer. She proved to be of great assistance by helping him recover from the wound and his other disabilities brought about by the loss of an eye, malaria and other things.

Captain Locker, now Lieut-Governor at Greenwich, a great friend and one time colleague met with Nelson at this period and was somewhat shocked at his appearance. Earlier a portrait had been painted of him when he was in the full glow of health. Now Locker suggested that his appearance and promotion merited a new painting. Nelson was eventually convinced. He agreed to sit for a new portrait. The artist, Lemuel Abbott was commissioned and started sittings. The portrait is now preserved at Greenwich, and can be compared with others made earlier. His illnesses and wounding make him appear even to this day, upright but with greying hair. His face has not lost the look of authority, but certainly is marked, and very care worn and weathered.. His youth has fled, but not his bold spirit.

On 29th March 1798, Rear Admiral Sir Horatio Nelson rejoined his Flag Ship the ten-year-old 'Vanguard' of seventy four guns, and she sailed down the Channel to the tip of the Isle of Wight en route to the Atlantic. He was on his way to the Mediterranean again, to Malta, Gozo, Greece and to the ports close to Egypt. He was aware that a large contingent of French vessels had sailed through that area. It was an intelligence he obtained from merchant shipping anxious to help the British cause. He knew that Napoleon Bonaparte was not far away. He was not wrong and in a short time the lookouts had spotted the masts of the French fleet which had been headed by their Admiral into the bay of Alexandria. The great Battle of the Nile was to take place just before Nelson's birthday when he would be forty years of age.

History books have related the details of the battle of the Nile. It was an outstanding victory in which Nelson was again wounded, this time again in the head. The victory achieved at the Nile was remarkable and the day after the battle was marked by Nelson ordering that the domestic tasks such as 'swabbing the decks' should be left until after a service had been held in remembrance of those who had lost their lives in action.

At this moment Nelson was told that his subordinate officers, in other words his fellow Officers were to commission a presentation sword, and a portrait to hang in the premises of the Egyptian Club which they had formed. The expression in itself is harmless enough and no inference should be drawn from this that Nelson was a Freemason. This will be discussed at a later stage with other allusions which are pertinent.

It is interesting to remark however, that at the Battle of the Nile, Nelson called his fellow Officers together in his cabin, the floor of which was 'carpeted' by a piece of sailcloth marked out in black and white squares. This interesting floor covering is still to be seen in the 'Victory', to which it must have been transferred by order of Nelson himself.

The victory over the French Fleet had been terrible, bloody, and decisive. The news of this victory was sent by dispatch to the Admiralty but was slow in reaching London, however when it did, the joy and happiness knew no bounds.

Nelson was now 'The Hero of the Nile'. More was to follow for he was created 'Baron Nelson of the Nile and Burnham Thorpe. His finances also were uplifted by the grant of a pension of £2000 per annum, whilst his agent worked hard to make sure that he was rewarded by his share of the 'Prize Money' awarded for the capture of French ships either in the Battle or singly whilst at sea.

He was as yet not able to return to England, for he was ordered to do additional duties in relation to the blockade of Malta and it was necessary for him to go to Naples.

In Naples he was again welcomed by Sir William and Lady Hamilton who not only celebrated with him the great victory, but also arranged a huge birthday party in his honour. It is sad to recall, that at this time, as his relationship with Lady Hamilton became more intimate, his letters to his wife indicate a deterioration and bitterness.

When the time came for him to set out for England, he did so in company with the Hamiltons, the journey being made by crossing Europe now at peace and making for Hamburg. At this point a British Frigate should have been there to have met them, but as this did not happen, they travelled on in a mail boat named 'The King George' which landed them in Great Yarmouth, Norfolk. It was 6th November 1800.

He had written his instructions to Fanny giving a clear indication of the type of house and home he wanted and further she was told to buy a small but comfortable carriage.

However, he was detained in Great Yarmouth by Civic ceremonies at which he stated, "I am a Norfolk man, and glory in being so". He took the opportunity of visiting a Norfolk Church where they played 'See the Conquering Hero comes', and whilst the invitations included his wife, she remained in London. She was not to know, that he had already written to the Admiralty asking for an immediate return to active duty. When he did return, the house in Dover Street which they were renting was not ready. They therefore had to remain in an hotel named Nerot's Hotel. Shortly after, Nelson introduced his wife to Sir William and Lady Hamilton who then travelled on to their own house in Grosvenor Square. Emma was at this time pregnant, a fact which could hardly be concealed. His wife had hoped that

Nelson would return to being the loving, and generous man she remembered from their marriage. Unfortunately this was not to be and Fanny reconciled herself to the fact that the time would come when Nelson would leave. When he did, the news became the 'talking point' of London society. Malicious gossip, newspaper articles, and lampooning cartoons caused many who were friends to turn their backs on Nelson and Lady Hamilton, and society almost forgot their existence.

There is no doubt that this period of Nelson's life must be regarded as one of religion and reflection. He was in love, but above every thing else, he wished and wanted to get back to his very active life in the Navy. The lonely existence now brought back memories of his strict up-bringing by his father. Nevertheless, he consoled himself by regarding the union with Emma Hamilton as a spiritual marriage. In a letter to her, he addressed her as "my own dear wife, for such you are in my eyes and in the face of heaven". He had by now broken with Fanny, and one morning he left her never to return to their dwelling except for one occasion. Fanny asked him then, if she had ever given cause for complaint. His reply was a definite negative, and with that they parted. The legal formalities of the marriage were all that now remained.

As if a bell had sounded in the Admiralty, Nelson was now appointed second in command of the Channel Fleet and further elevated to the rank of Vice-Admiral. This promotion being effective from 1st January 1801. His flagship was one that he indeed was responsible for capturing four years earlier at Cape St. Vincent. It was the 'San Josef'. With his flag established and flying, he made to sea, leaving behind the scandal and bawdy wit generated by those who found humour in the situation with Emma Hamilton. Whilst Nelson was moving to take over his new command, Emma gave birth to a daughter who would be named Horatia, it was 5th February 1801.

Seven days later, Nelson transferred from the 'San Josef' to the 'St. George'. It was in this vessel that he left to join Admiral Sir Hyde Parker at Great Yarmouth.

Rear Admiral Sir Horatio Nelson.

A portrait painted by Lemuel Francis Abbott (1760-1803).

Probably the most famous portrait painted in 1798-9 after the Nile from an earlier sketch. The artist did not know that Nelson's head wound meant that he could only wear his hat tipped off his fore-head, and had to guess at the chelenk's appearance.

(Reproduced by kind permission of the National Maritime Museum at Greenwich.)

We should now read a report contained in the 'Quatuor Coronati Lodge' Transactions Vol.69 of 1956, pages 127-132. Written by Brother A. Stuart Brown entitled 'The Gregorians in Norfolk'. It is part of the evidence to be considered: "The next known Grand of the Norwich 'Gregorians' is William Gooch Pillans Esq of Bracondale, Norwich. It was during his tenure of the Office of Grand that Lord Nelson was admitted to the 'Gregorian Order'. On 2nd March 1801, Lord Nelson sailed into Yarmouth Roads in command of a squadron of seven ships of the line and flying his Flag on the 'St. George', there to join the Fleet in charge of Admiral Sir Hyde Parker. On 12th March the Fleet sailed to attack Copenhagen."

"During his stay in Yarmouth Roads, Nelson wrote a letter to Mr Pillans Grand of the Gregorians, in thanks for his admission to that Society." It is also known that Lady Nelson wrote acknowledging the safe receipt of the Lord Nelson's Regalia which had been sent to her.

The Battle of Copenhagen was again, a battle of tactics, at which Nelson was pre-eminent. The bombardment carried out by the men of war, and the skilful placement of these vessels, together with the anchorage, enabled an advantage to be gained. A truce was agreed, allowing for discussions to take place between the two sides. Eventually agreement was reached and an armistice was signed.

The stories concerning Nelson have been added to, by an account given by one of his officers who had pointed out a signal made by the Commander in Chief requiring the attacking forces to 'fall back'. Nelson could see no sense in falling back, when a definite advantage had been won. With the signal before him, he was supposed to have put the telescope to his blinded eye, and said, "Really Foley, I have only one eye and have a right to be blind sometimes, I really do not see the signal". In the meantime, during the round table conference, news was conveyed to the Danes, that a group of Russian Officers had murdered the Russian Czar. The documents for Peace were signed at once. The Baltic war was ended. It had been a great and glorious battle, combining all of the arts of sea warfare, and in the latter stages, the true skill of diplomatic effort. Nelson was rewarded for these efforts by being elevated to the rank of a Viscount, shortly afterwards he became Commander in Chief. There can be no doubt that the part played by Nelson in dealing with the Baltic wars had marked him down, not only as a very capable senior Officer in the Navy, but in the long negotiations to conclude the Armistice he played a vital diplomatic role which was recognised by those on both sides of the table. The years which were to follow, that is from 1801 and 1802 were for the main part, full of alarms and excursions.

The alarms were caused by the actions of the French on the continent. It was thought at one time that Napoleon was considering the possibility of invading Britain. Nelson argued that to be able to do that, the French would have to cross the channel. The British Navy could not, and would not, let that happen. He stated, "I feel confident that the fleets of our enemy will meet the same fate which has always attended them". On 27th July 1801, he hoisted his flag in the 'Unite', a former French frigate, and in that ship he headed a small fleet of some thirty ships towards the Kentish Coast. To be so near to the French Coast was a spur to action, so he decided to sail across to Boulogne. Once there he was confronted with a line of barges and other obstructions, and, not wishing to be be-calmed, he ordered his bomb ketches 'to go in nearer and throw a few explosive shells amongst the gathered ships and defences and then to sail clear'. This preliminary skirmish was the fore-runner of a greater effort for which the French were better prepared, and resulted in the British fleet losing a number of men killed without any advantage gained. It was a bitter blow for Nelson.

At this time, Emma Hamilton informed him by letter that she had found him a house at Merton in the South West of London and near the Portsmouth Road. He wrote to her from Deal immediately before going to Flushing on reconnaissance saying, "I approve of the house at Merton". The date was the

20th August but it was not until the end of August that Nelson returned from his sea voyages. He was still on board on 21st October, but realised that within a day or two he would be on his way to London and to Merton. In fact he made his way ashore at Deal, travelled through one day and night, and arrived at Merton early on the morning of the third day. It was a happy and joyous time for the whole family and especially for Emma Hamilton.

In the period of the next three years, and before being fully recalled to the Navy, Nelson had much to occupy his mind. He was, after all, now a Member of the House of Lords, and would be required to take his seat. He would from time to time join in the debates, and after his maiden speech, his colleagues congratulated him for his understanding of the situation. When at Merton, he would from time to time enjoy the pastime of fishing which he did in the local River Wandle. It was a pleasure for him to walk in the surrounding countryside and local farmlands. He was at peace with the world in the realisation that on 1st October 1801 The Treaty of Amiens was signed which formally ended hostilities between Britain and France.

His happiness was marred in the early part of the next year by the death of his father on 26th April and the loss of his spiritual guide and mentor caused him great distress. It was not the only death to affect him, for within a short time Sir William Hamilton passed away. Nelson was with him at his passing, and it is not surprising to learn that he died in his wife's arms with Nelson holding his hand. His last words left Emma to Nelson's protection, and prayed that justice should be done to her for the many services she had rendered to Britain.

Shortly after, war between Britain and France was declared again. On 18th May, 1803 the King's message was read to the Houses of Parliament. Nelson left immediately to take command of the Mediterranean fleet. On that same 18th May, Nelson hoisted his flag on the 'Victory', and on 6th July he joined the fleet off Toulon. He was aware that the month of August was the most likely when the French would try to cross the English Channel in an invasion attempt. By blocking the French ports he therefore could prevent such an attempt and cause the whole scheme to founder. Added to the worries of the Nation at this time was the fact that Spain had also declared war on Britain. Napoleon visualised the fact that, if the two fleets of France and Spain could unite, it would give him a sufficient strength and advantage to go ahead with his invasion plan.

The years 1803 and 1804 were 'Cat and the Mouse' years. There were periods when Nelson was making tours in this country, which from a public relations point of view did much to raise the morale of the people. Many of these Local Government tours were related to the manufacturers of equipment used by the navy. On the other hand he visited the University of Oxford and had an Honorary Degree bestowed upon him. From Oxford he commenced a Welsh tour via the Forest of Dean, Ross on Wye and thence to Monmouth where he stayed for two nights. He was entertained most Royally. Early one morning he was taken by coach to the top of Kymin Hill. He was aware that a Temple had been built in honour of those Officers and Men who had fought against the French at the Battle of the Nile. The mural depicting this Victory, he was not able to see, but at one of the receptions he spoke highly of it and promised that 'He would always do his duty in the tradition of those whose memory was recalled'. His journey continued to Hereford where he was again honoured by being given the Freedom of the town of Hereford. Having completed the journey across Wales, he travelled to Worcester, Birmingham and Warwick, before finally returning to London.

He spent most of the spring and summer of 1803 in attending to matters of personal accounts and visiting their Lordships at the Admiralty. One personal matter he attended was the baptism of his daughter Horatia in the Parish Church at St. Marylebone. Christened Horatia Nelson Thompson, she was just two and a half years of age. Nelson left afterwards for Portsmouth where he was to take over a most powerful vessel which would be his flagship. It was the 'Victory'.

It is not necessary to pursue the details which occupied Nelson in the months which were to pass, sufficient to say that letters poured from his pen to Emma, and amongst other things was a detailed study of Mediterranean strategy. His duty lay in keeping the French fleet in port, and should any venture out they should be captured or destroyed.

There is little doubt that his greatest worry was his own personal health. He had good reasons to thank his own personal servant Tom Allen. Nelson was in pain, but Tom Allen looked after him by taking and keeping him away from the circulating wine bottle. He summed the state of his health up by expressing, "I really believe that my shatter'd carcase is in the worst plight of the whole fleet". He was suffering from a form of rheumatic fever which with his other wounds was causing pain to him generally. His eyesight was diminishing and he was afraid of going blind. He needed a rest away from the Navy, and so, arriving off Gibraltar 20th July 1805, he went ashore for the first time since June 1803. He continued onwards to London for a short stay, and then headed for his beloved Merton where he arrived early in the morning of 22nd August. For the next ten days, he was 'at home' and enjoyed the peace and tranquility which had been prepared for him, together with his guests by Lady Hamilton. He was able to visit London, where he was immediately recognised in every place that he visited. Merton, of course was a visit of remembrance, here were the people he loved and with them, he made the most of the days available to him. On the morning of 2nd September, at five a.m. a carriage arrived in which a young Captain was travelling to London with despatches. It was Captain Henry Blackwood who had stopped to inform Nelson that the combined French and Spanish Fleets were assembled in Cadiz Harbour.

He left for London at once where he was to meet the First Sea Lord and also the Prime Minister, Mr William Pitt. The die was cast, with The Prime Minister insisting that he should take Command, and be ready to leave in three days. The first Lord of the Admiralty insisted also that he should choose his own

Officers to command. Back in Merton, he attended to the accounts and discussed the gardens with Cribb the gardener. He invited certain persons to dine with him and even went to the local school where he heard the boys doing their recitations. With Emma he shared a ceremony of Communion at which rings were exchanged. The next morning he drove from Merton, and after changing horses at Liphook, he continued, to arrive in Portsmouth just before dawn. Even at that early hour, there were huge crowds to cheer him and to see him off. To try and avoid these, they had the Admiral's Barge sent to the beach at Southsea where he boarded. The crowds there cheered, and as he sat down, after waving his hat to them, he turned to Thomas Hardy and remarked, "I have had their Huzzas before, now I have their hearts". The crowd replied with 'Three United Cheers'.

On 14th September he re-boarded the 'Victory' and set sail on the next day. He arrived off Cadiz on the 27th. All necessary precautions, not to alert the enemy of his arrival in the 'Victory' had been taken. The arrival of their Commander in Chief was welcomed by the Captains. Two days later, it was Nelson's birthday, and to celebrate his 47th Birthday, invitations to dinner aboard the 'Victory' had been sent to fifteen of his Captains. This bore in some measure a similarity to events which took place at the Battle of the Nile. On that occasion, 'The Band of Brothers' were invited to meet Nelson, and the strategy of the Battle was decided. Now, once again before a major sea engagement takes place, he invited them to come aboard to the Birthday party, where no doubt, he laid before them the plan he had prepared for attacking the enemy. There were one or two minor matters which excited his attention. He communicated with Emma and told her that 'The Nelson Touch' was approved by his Captains.

Nelsons long wait was nearly over. He had chased Villeneuve over to the West Indies after he got out from Toulon. He had returned, and now Battle was about to be joined, when on 18th October the French Fleet put to sea. The frigate commanded by

Henry Blackwood was keeping a watchful eye on the movements of the French and Spanish ships, and directly communicated these to the 'Victory'. Nelson decided to clear his desk, and prepared a document recommending the Government to bequeath a pension on Emma, Lady Hamilton in return for the services she had rendered to Britain whilst in Naples. He asked Hardy and Blackwood to witness and sign the document, and then with these two officers he completed a quick examination of the ship and went to the Quarter Deck. He was reported to be in excellent 'spirits' and had laughed and joked with his crew. He then returned to his cabin where he wrote a letter to Emma. On the bare boards of the cabin he knelt and offered a prayer.

"May the Great God whom I worship grant to my Country and for the benefit of Europe in general, a great and glorious victory; and may no misconduct in anyone tarnish it, and may humanity after Victory be the dominant feature in the British Fleet. For myself, individually, I commit my Life to Him who made me, and may His blessings light upon my endeavours for serving my Country faithfully. To Him I resign myself and the just cause which is entrusted to me to defend. Amen Amen Amen."

After writing this prayer he also dictated to the signals Lieutenant, John Pascoe, a signal which he wished to address to the whole fleet, it was "ENGLAND CONFIDES THAT EVERY MAN WILL DO HIS DUTY". However, after discussion with Pascoe it was amended to read:

"ENGLAND EXPECTS THAT EVERY MAN WILL DO HIS DUTY".

It was a signal that touched the heart of every man in every vessel in the fleet and was loudly acclaimed.

THE BATTLE OF TRAFALGAR
21st OCTOBER 1805

History books written by experts in Naval warfare will explain in detail the skill employed over a period of time, on the date above, to make this Glorious Victory complete. Every schoolboy must know that at the height of the battle Admiral Lord Nelson was shot down and some four hours later, after hearing from Captain Hardy that the victory had been gained, Nelson died. His death was carefully recorded in the ship's log.

The Battle was over and the victory won. The battleship 'Victory' was taken in tow for return to England calling first at Gibraltar. Nelson's body had been stripped of clothes, the head had been shaved and all hair cut off as he had ordered, and then the body had been placed in a barrel of Brandy. At Gibraltar the body was transferred to a lead lined coffin which was filled with spirits of wine, camphor and myrrh. The 'Victory' was towed past the ships of the Channel Fleet and anchored for a time at Spithead. It then moved on to Greenwich where the coffin was then encased in another lead Coffin, and then the outer wooden coffin was sealed around it. Nelson's own sailors rowed the Admiral's Barge bearing the sealed Coffin up the river to the Whitehall Steps. At this point it was taken from the Barge to a room at the Admiralty, which even to this day is known as 'The Nelson Room'.

The next day, 9th January 1806 the state funeral at St. Paul's Cathedral took place and Nelson was laid to rest directly beneath the Cross of the church in a tomb in the crypt.

Now we must examine the evidence which from time to time arises concerning Freemasonry. The question is asked very often by persons interested in History.

"WAS HORATIO, LORD NELSON, A FREEMASON".

In an 'Appendix' to a book published in 1896, entitled 'A

History of Freemasonry in Norfolk', the author quotes an article which appeared in the Freemason's Quarterly Review for 1839, Page 440. It simply states that: Nelson and Tom Allen, his personal servant, were both Masons. No evidence was produced to justify such an assertion. In fact quite the reverse. At that time the Sub-Librarian of the Grand Lodge, was Bro. Henry Sadler, a very thorough, and meticulous researcher, who said that he had not been able to find either of these names in the registers. In particular, he had made a special search of all the lists of Norfolk Lodges. Those Lodges, most popular amongst Naval Officers, were also critically examined without any reference being found to Nelson being admitted as a Mason.

Then, in the search for the correct answer to the question, on three separate occasions the registers of the two Grand Lodges in existence, prior to the union, have been searched. The name of Nelson, under any of his styles or titles has not been found.

Whilst researching this question, considerable time has been spent in the British Library where there are a vast quantities of books written about him. I support the statement of my great friend and colleague, the Grand Librarian John Hamill, that none of them have mentioned or claimed him to be a Freemason.

Amongst other questions asked, is one relative to his membership of the Union Lodge No.331 in York. The reply by Bro. John Hamill is comprehensive and is as follows: The Union Lodge No.331, York is still in existence. What has happened is due to the passage of time and the system of closing the Lodge numbers up as other Lodges have handed in their warrants and been lost for ever by closing. Union Lodge of York held No.331 from 1792-1814, when it became No.423. It was at this time that the Union of the Grand Lodges took place, and the Registers of the Grand Lodges were then combined. The Lodge initially became No.287. In the year 1832, a further closing up finally gave it the number No.236. So much for the Number, and we now learn of a further change. A petition was received in 1870 seeking and requesting a 'Change in the name of the Lodge' from 'Union' to 'York'. The change was approved and it remains now as York Lodge No.236. Warranted in 1777, the minute books have been carefully preserved and are still in existence. Reference is made on one occasion only to Lord Nelson. On 16th December 1805, the Lodge resolved, 'to hold a public procession which was deemed to take place on the interment of our departed Hero and Brother Lord Nelson'. A mourning banner was made and still hangs in the Masonic Hall, Dunscombe Place, York. It bears the words, 'We rejoice with our Country but mourn for our Brother'. The Funeral of Lord Nelson took place on 9th January 1806, in a most disciplined and ordered ceremony. The final interment taking place in the crypt of St. Paul's Cathedral . The 'Mourning Banner', may well have been used at a service organised by the Master of the Lodge, to mark the love and esteem with which they, and countless other persons throughout the country, held the late Admiral.

The 'Nelson Stone' which will always be mentioned in connection with Nelson and Freemasonry is held by the Lodge of United Friends No.564. The Lodge was constituted on 11th August A.D. 1797, and it holds in its possession a block of white marble about the size of a house brick. On one side is carved the Name of the Lodge and the date of constitution and then there are carved the names of the Junior and Senior Wardens, together with the name of the Lodge Secretary. It would appear that the name of the Master has been removed. On the other side a Memorial Notice is carved stating as follows:

In Memory of Bror. Vt NELSON
Of the Nile, & of Burnham Thorpe in
Norfolk, who lost his life in the arms
of Victory, in an engagement with ye
Combin'd Fleets of France & Spain,
of Cape Trafalgar, Oct, 21. 1805.
Proposed by Bro. John Cutlove.

John Cutlove was a Mason who was initiated into the Lodge of United Friends No.564 on 12th April 1799. The Proposal by Bro. Cutlove cannot intend that he was proposing Nelson into the Lodge, but merely giving voice to a national feeling of melancholy and reserve at losing such a fine man. He wanted his fellow masons to agree that the loss should be remarked and remembered.

The term 'Brothers' is used very widely and does not signify that all of Nelson's fellow Officers were, or had, a Masonic inclination.

The Nelson Crimson Oakes Medallion, which can be seen in the Grand Lodge Library again raises some thought, but it is more likely to be connected with a Benefit Society many of which were started after Nelson's death. Very little if anything remains of them today, and one can only conclude that they were started with not the highest of ideals. The use of Nelson's name and memory, may well have been an inducement to join, and part with a certain amount of 'Charitable' money. The use of symbols illustrated on the medallion was in keeping with some of the quasi masonic groups which have long since disappeared.

It has also been remarked that Masons in Cork, Ireland meet together on Trafalgar Day and they have no doubts that Nelson was a Mason. With all of the evidence before us we can only say with some certainty that Admiral Lord Nelson was admitted into the Society of Gregorians whilst visiting Great Yarmouth. His letter to the Secretary of that Organisation is proof. His wife's letter to the same man acknowledged receipt of his regalia. Lodges abroad have been consulted, including those in Malta, the records in the Grand Lodge Library have been minutely scanned, Greenwich, Monmouth, the British Library, Portsmouth, and Norfolk have all been the subject of close enquiry. Finally there is in the Museum and Library of Westminster Abbey a remarkable wax effigy of Horatio Lord Nelson. So lifelike is this figure that Emma, Lady Hamilton wanted to kiss the lips. She was restrained from doing so, because the lips, which were painted with red paint were still wet.

There has been a feeling of great joy in doing this research, but when all is said and done the question still remains:

WAS ADMIRAL LORD NELSON A MASON?

To which the answer must be given!

NO.

NOT PROVEN!

APPENDIX No. 1

Fifty years ago on 18th October 1927, an Oration was given in Leith Lodge No.223 named the Trafalgar Lodge. The Oration was given by Bro. Andrew Wilson, Past Master of Lodge No.1 of Scotland, and Past Grand Bard on 'The Memory of Nelson'.

He said, "Once every year Lodge Trafalgar pauses in its labours and looks backwards to a great and glorious memory. Let us think what memory really means. It is obvious that without memory, we should work out our destiny like beasts of the field, guided by a blind instinct; but, because we can recall not only our own experiences, but also the experiences of others, we can begin to build where others have left off, and so mankind progresses materially, intellectually and spiritually.

Memory, however, is more than a mere mechanical recalling of the past. Properly used, memory has a selective and refining quality. You have all had some great sorrow, a loss, a disappointment, a bereavement. At the time the pain was almost unbearable; but memory has smoothed the aching pain, covered up what was ugly or evil, and left only the good to shine out of the past.

When the curtain of time is rolled aside, and we understand the source of all our gifts, it is possible that we may find that the meaning of the phrase the "forgiveness of sins" is that the Great Architect has given us memories like His own, and that the much evil we have done will be forgotten and the good which is in us will be remembered. In that spirit let us look back tonight when we honour the memory of Nelson.

The Orator then went on to discuss the History of Nelson from the time that he first joined the Navy, through the various sea battles until finally he outlined the great victory at Trafalgar. In this great moment Nelson, mortally wounded exclaimed "Thank God, I have done my duty".

There one might stop but for the duty laid on one who tells the story of Trafalgar to tell the fruits of victory. Nelson's dying utterance was not a personal satisfaction with his life. He knew how he had accomplished a great task. Two hundred thousand Frenchmen had been waiting at Boulogne to invade England. The menace of this invasion was very real. A few hundred yards from here the old grey Martello Tower stands to remind us of it. Nelson knew that he had rendered the invasion of England impossible by securing the command of the seas. Not an enemy ship engaged at the Battle of Trafalgar ever put to sea again. That was the duty that he had done, and before he died he knew the importance of his victory. He did not know, however, that he had gathered into his own personality all the finest traditions of the Navy and the sea, and that his memory would not only be an inspiration to all who go down to the sea in ships, but also be a glorious example to us all of simple strong religion, triumph of spirit over physical suffering, loyalty to those under us, courage, thoroughness in doing our duty, the Divine quality of mercy, and that heroism and self sacrifice which enable a man to pass through death, the gate of life with the sure knowledge that death hath no terror comparable to the stain of falsehood and dishonour.

BRETHREN, WILL YOU RISE? I ask you to drink proudly, gratefully and in reverent silence to:

THE MEMORY OF NELSON.

APPENDIX No. 2
NELSONIC CRIMSON OAKES

In my search for detail for this current paper, my attention was drawn to a paper prepared in the Grand Lodge Library in March 1983 and initialled T.O.H. This paper is here re-produced by kind permission of the Grand Librarian W.Bro. John Hamill whose help as ever has been generously given.
Information leaflet No.19.

Apart from the existence of a number of examples of the medal illustrated on the next page very little is known about this Order. The Library and Museum has, over a number of years, tried to obtain information but without success. The medal is listed in the British Museum Catalogue but that Museum has not been able to furnish any details about the Order itself.

In all probability the Nelsonic Crimson Oakes was a Friendly or Benefit Society of the sort that existed in considerable numbers at the end of the 18th and into the 19th centuries. According to the inscription on the Medal it came into being on the 19th January 1808 and it could well be that its name [and others like it – see below] was inspired by the patriotic fervour aroused by the death of Nelson on 21st October 1805.

Although there are Masonic references to Nelson as 'our departed Brother and Hero' etc. no firm evidence has ever been found in Grand Lodge Records – or elsewhere – to prove that he was a member of the Craft. Freemasonry did not, and does not, have a monopoly of the designation 'brother' and it could well be that in the circumstances of mourning for a national hero its use in connection with Nelson was in the general, humane sense [compare, for instance, the similar wording of the Anglican funeral service].

An announcement in an [unidentified] Birmingham newspaper of 12th August 1811 stated that the first anniversary of the 'Lodge of the Most Noble Order of Nelsonic Oakes' would be held at the Star Inn, High Street, Stourbridge on 21st August 1811. The Grand Lodge Library has a handwritten summons for a meeting of 'Lord Nelson's Benefit Society' at the Golden Bell, Portsmouth, on 28th November 1831. It also has in its files a parchment document, seemingly a membership certificate, issued on behalf of a body calling itself the 'Grand National Lodge [of] Nelsonian Arkwrights and Mariners' which, according to the imprint 'Was established in London, October 21 AD 1812'. The text of this certificate is inscribed by hand in a cypher which, when decoded, is couched in high-sounding terms making little sense. None of these organisations was Masonic and it is impossible now to say whether they were connected in any way with the Nelsonic Crimson Oakes.

The medal which is reproduced to actual size on this page was struck in silver or white metal; it is 53mm in diameter. The medallist may possibly have been Bendetto Pistrucci [1784-1855] on the evidence of the initials 'B P' which appear on some examples on the edge of Nelson's epaulette. Pistrucci came to England in 1815 and in 1828 was appointed chief medallist at the Royal Mint. A member of the medals and coins department of Spink and Son Ltd., to whom one of the Grand Lodge Museum's examples was shown [Sept 1970] gave his opinion that the medal was 'more than likely' by Pistrucci but was not prepared to confirm this as a complete certainty. The fact that the medal bears symbols which happen also to be used in Freemasonry does not in this instance, as in many others, point to a Masonic connection. Many friendly societies and convivial clubs made use, [some of the former still do] of emblems and symbols similar to, or even identical, with those used in Freemasonry, and in other respects they often borrowed from, or modelled themselves on the craft system, [the Ancient Order of Gregorian for example, of which it is known that Nelson was elected a member]. The Cross and Anchor, seen on the Nelsonic Crimson Oakes medal, are in any case themselves age-old symbols of Faith and Hope occurring universally in Christian iconography before adoption into that of Freemasonry.

Masonic Chart 1. Sea chest on HMS Victory early 1800s.

44

APPENDIX No. 3
THE SEA CHEST ON HMS 'VICTORY'

Havant in Hants is not far from Portsmouth, and it is there that W.Bro. Jack Barrett lives.

He regularly attends at the Quatuor Coronati Lodge Meetings and indeed I am indebted to him for some interesting information concerning a sea chest which is on the middle deck of the 'Victory' and near to the Quartermaster. It is only right to put things into perspective, for Jack Barrett in his working life was Superintendent Electrical Engineer for the Portsmouth Dockyards and was often to be found aboard Nelson's Flag Ship either in connection with his work, and on those splendid social occasions which from time to time are held 'on board'.

The sea chest is not large but on opening the chest there is to be found a Masonic chart. It is painted in water colours and is approximately 2ft x 1ft 6 ins in size. It is obviously 'home made', and from the nature of the design, an age can also be visualised as being early 18th century. The early history of the chest, or the

Masonic Chart 2. Sea chest on HMS Victory early 1800s.

purpose to which it was put are not known, and the chart has to be deemed as a personal record made by the owner of the chest. It is unlikely that Masonic Meetings took place on the 'Victory'.

Near to the top of the chart and on each side is a red cross surrounded by a sash, whilst on either side of the sash is a WHITE and RED ENSIGN. [Probably a memory of the Red and White Fleets.] Above each and in the centre are pairs of Hearts. In the centre also are drawn a pair of clasped hands, to which the Artist has added another pair of hands holding a bunch of grapes.

The bottom half of this chart can be deemed as Masonic. Illustrated are the square paving, a coffin, and the three lesser lights. Between the lights, the moon is illustrated surrounded with seven stars, also the sun with a face and radiating points. On each side is a fluted column, garlanded with roses and surmounted with a globe. Other illustrations include a sprig of acacia, a beehive, two keys, and a church with a retaining wall. Between the columns are five steps with an arch resting on two columns, also the square and compasses supporting a letter 'G' within a triangle.

Three rather faint figures probably represent FAITH, HOPE, and CHARITY or LOVE.

FAITH on the right holds a Chalice with a cross above it, in her left hand is a book presumably a Bible.

HOPE, opposite is an almost invisible figure, and would have had an anchor.

CHARITY or LOVE above the Arch is represented by a Lady with a child in her arms and surrounded by a nimbus

Red and Blue are used extensively especially on the steps, columns, and the squared pavement. The arched area spanning the pavement with a star and could represent a vault. Who knows what the artist had in mind, and the more important thought exists. Was he trying to convey to those who followed him that he was also a Companion of the Holy Royal Arch.

This we shall never know, but it serves to illustrate one point. Admiral the Lord Nelson was not a Mason himself, but research could be undertaken to determine if any of those who served with him or under him were indeed Members of the Craft.

46

APPENDIX No. 4

An article which has appeared in the 1997 Year Book of the 'Friends of the Royal Naval Museum and HMS Victory', poses the question 'Was Nelson a Mason?'.

The Author of the Article will not object if his attention is drawn to certain wrong premises.

Quote: "Freemasonry has been in the news for the past few months". This is quite correct since there was a Home Office Committee formed to discuss certain aspects of the Craft.. The following observation was one of their conclusions. "We do not believe that there is anything sinister about Freemasonry, properly observed, and are confident that Freemasonry itself does not encourage malpractice.

It is not correct to say that it is an all male preserve. For many years now, there has been a women's organisation with their own Grand Lodge, and Lodges which meet throughout the country. Their work and ideals are well recognised as charitable and helpful in society.

Having said that I am pleased to see in the article the short extract from a letter written to Mrs Nesbit just before her marriage to Nelson, dated 28th February 1787 from 'Boreal'. In this letter Nelson details the appointments which he anticipates keeping, the extract reads 'In the evening we attend a Freemason's Ball. Tuesday, Please God we sail'.

This extract does not intend that Nelson was a Mason. Many persons attend Masonic functions and most Lodges have a 'Ladies Night' once or twice a year. They promote the cause of supporting Charities and bring a great feeling of 'Togetherness' to the Members and their respective wives.

The other points have been dealt with in the main document.

THE EPILOGUE

Nelson was buried in St. Paul's Cathedral on the 9th day of January 1806.

The funeral service lasted approximately four hours and included the ceremony of the breaking of the staves by the King at Arms who also proclaimed the styles, titles and dignities of the deceased Peer. A group of sailors who had served on the 'Victory', bore into the Cathedral the ensigns of the famous ship, and spontaneously tore the largest ensign into pieces so that they might retain a memory of their Commander whose body was being laid to rest.

Garter King at Arms, Sir Isaac Heard, then announced the following styles and titles as follows:

"Thus it has pleased Almighty God to take, out of this transitory life, unto his divine mercy, the Most Noble Lord Horatio Nelson, Viscount and Baron Nelson of the Nile, and of Burnham Thorpe, in the County of Norfolk, Baron Nelson of the Nile, and of Hillborough in the same County; Knight of the Most Honourable Order of the Bath; Vice-Admiral of the White Squadron of the Fleet, and Commander in Chief of His Majesty's ships and vessels in the Mediterranean; also Duke of Bronte in Sicily; Knight Grand Cross of the Sicillian Order of St. Ferdinand and of Merit; Member of the Ottoman Order of the Crescent; Knight Grand Commander of the Order of St. Joachim; and the Hero who, in the moment of victory, fell covered with immortal glory. Let us humbly trust that he is now raised to bliss ineffable and to a glorious immortality!

When at 5.33 in the afternoon the coffn was lowered into the crypt of St. Paul's Cathedral, it was laid in a black marble sarcophagus originally made for Cardinal Wolsey by Roverzano before 1530. However after the dispute between the Cardinal and Henry the Eighth, when he was expelled from the court, the sarcophagus was confiscated by the King. Here Nelson rests and close to hand are the memorials of many who not only served with him but were his closest friends.

The memory of Nelson is preserved in countless ways. The most widely known is of course the effigy of Nelson which stands on the column in Trafalgar Square. It is 145 feet above the pavement of Trafalgar Square and Nelson is looking down Whitehall towards the Admiralty. On the 21st day of October when evening falls many dinners take place to 'remember' the victory which Nelson gained and the toast on these occasions is always to 'The Immortal Memory'.

Nelson cannot be remembered as a Freemason, but the rector of the church which his father presided over in Burnham Thorpe, in one memorial service, summed the whole thing up in an improvised prayer which ended in this fashion.

'And we thank thee, O Lord, for the life of Horatio Nelson and for his services to HUMANITY.'

THE TOMB OF ADMIRAL LORD NELSON IN THE CRYPT OF ST. PAUL'S CATHEDRAL.

Nelson was laid to rest in the tomb prepared for him in the crypt of St Paul's Cathedral on the 9th day of January 1806. The Sarcophagus was originally made for Cardinal Wolsey before 1530 by Rovezzano. However, when the cardinal was expelled from the court the sarcophagus was taken from him by order of King Henry the Eighth. Some of the memorials in the surrounding area are of men who fought with Nelson at Trafalgar and at Copenhagen.

BIBLIOGRAPHY

Since the death of Admiral Lord Nelson, followed by the great funeral at St. Paul's Cathedral on the 9th January 1806, there have been literally hundreds of books published concerning Nelson, his life as a boy and the starting of his career in the Royal Navy. Many of these book were written at a time just after the Battle of Trafalgar, whilst others deal with the tactics employed in his great sea battles. On the other hand there are many written concerning the numerous letters written by him to his wife and to Lady Hamilton, whilst others, written by Officers who served under the Lord Nelson relate stories and happenings describing his love for the sea and his respect for his Officers and men.

It is impossible to contemplate a book or writing about Nelson without due reference to:

1. The British Library in London, who as I write this short note are moving their collection a short distance away to another headquarters.

2. The National Maritime Museum at Greenwich. A vast and interesting display was put on exhibition during 1997 and the visit is very worthwhile to view the excellent portraits of Nelson and others.

3. The Royal Naval Museum at Portsmouth where there is another portrait of Lord Nelson together with a collection of relative papers.

There is also a Museum at Monmouth where they hold the Llangattock Papers, and where in the church is part of the mainmast of the 'L'Orient' presented to St. Katherine's by Nelson.

My own reading took in those books available to me at the British Library, but I would most strongly represent to my Masonic friends three which particularly held my attention for detail and presentation they were:

(A). 'Nelson' by Carola Oman (London 1947).

(B). 'Horatio Nelson' by Tom Pocock (London 1987).

(C). 'Nelson, a personal History' by Christopher Hibbert. An excellent Penguin Book published in 1994.

ACKNOWLEDGEMENTS

I would like to say 'Thank You' to so many friends and others who have helped me to gather together the story of Horatio Nelson, and present it Masonic fashion.

There was Commander Hardy of the Portsmouth Installed Masters Lodge, who, after visiting that Lodge one evening invited me home and entertained me with stories and excellent Islay Whiskey whilst we looked over the plans or blue prints of the 'Victory'. No one could have known it better for at one time Cdr. Hardy had his Office on this famous ship.

The Librarian at St. Paul's Cathedral, Mr Joseph Wisdom M.A., A.L.A. who kindly sent me photocopies of the full description of the Funeral Service and interment of Lord Nelson which took place on 9th January 1806. It is a most moving document to read.

The Maritime Museum at Greenwich for their kindness in sending the details of the portraits they have hanging in the Museum, which in themselves are remarkable examples of the artists' work.

The photograph of the wax image of Lord Nelson was kindly sent by the Assistant Keeper of the Muniment Room and Library of Westminster Abbey. I wish to thank therefore, Mr R. Mortimer MA, PhD, FSA, FRHistS, for the kindness extended to me by the Assistant Keeper Miss Reynolds in forwarding to me the photograph of the wax effigy of Lord Nelson which can still be seen in the Museum at Westminster Abbey.

My thanks also go to Bro. Peter Racey of the Norfolk Installed Masters Lodge who like myself, is also fascinated by the 'Nelson' story. I am given to understand that he has written a Play about Lord Nelson which was performed in or near to Norwich.

Finally, last but by no means least, I acknowledge the considerable help given to me by the Grand Librarian Bro. John Hamill, and his staff, who are so understanding and helpful with advice and presentation to everyone, including casual visitors from all over the world, and those who like myself literally live quite close to Freemasons Hall.

I include also my great friend Charles Carter the Chief Executive of the Quatuor Coronati Lodge. No 2076. As usual, he reads the scripts through, and offers impartial advice to help the 'Poor Struggler' on his way. Thanks Charles and Jean.

DESCRIPTION OF THE FUNERAL CAR

THE following is an accurate description of the funeral car used at the obsequies of the late vice-admiral Horatio Viscount Nelson. It consists:

1stly. Of a platform, supported by springs upon a four-wheeled carriage, and decorated with black velvet drapery, and black fringe, in three large festoons, the centre of which, on both sides of the car, was inscribed with the word TRAFALGAR, in gold letters, and the exterior festoons were adorned with silver palm branches painted green, and glazed.

2ndly. Of another platform, raised upon the former, of the height of about eighteen inches, covered also with black velvet, ornamented with six escutcheons of his lordship's arms, impaling those of Viscountess Nelson, elegantly painted on satin, and alternated with laurel wreaths. Between the escutcheons were four scrolls surrounded by branches and wreaths of laurel (two on each side of the car), bearing the names of the four principal French and Spanish men of war, taken or destroyed by the lamented hero; namely – *San Josef, L'Orient, Trinidada, Bucentaure.*

3rdly. Of a third platform, on which the coffin was placed.

4thly. Of a canopy, in the shape of the upper part of an ancient sarcophagus, inscribed (on the upper part) in the front and summit of the cupola, over-hanging the spacious amphitheatre, covered also with black, as the place of interment. Nothing could have been more happily designed to gratify the anxious curiosity of the spectators, while it so effectually heightened the splendid solemnity of the scene.

The choir-service being ended, the temporary desk was removed to its place at the head of the grave, and a frame protruded from the grave by machinery in the vault, upon which the coffin was to rest whilst the remaining part of the burial service should be performing. The corpse was then brought back to the platform in procession, whilst a grand and solemn dirge, the composition of Mr Atwood, was played by that gentleman upon the organ. The Prince of Wales and his Royal Brothers assisted also in this procession. His Royal Highness, with the Duke of Clarence on his right and the Duke of Kent on his left, took his place in the platform on the right of the desk; and, with his royal and other attendants, stood during the whole service.

Here commenced the most impressive part of the spectacle, if not the most awful and affecting part of the whole ceremony. The coffin was uncovered, and the coronet placed on it: the moment was fast approaching, that was to consign to his last home the mortal remains of a consummate hero. The whole space of the platform was filled with those who had moved in the procession, as well as the passages surrounding the platform: the degree of light was sufficient to give effect to the splendour and magnificence of the scene, but not to afford a distinct view of its actual limits, so that the mind insensibly was impressed with that image of sublimity which belongs to infinity. The diversified dresses of the professional gentlemen that attended rendered the perspective highly pleasing, whilst the wavering of the different banners rendered it more beautiful and majestic.

At thirty-three minutes and a half past five precisely, the coffin was lowered into the grave, whither it was followed by the regrets of all that witnessed the affecting scene. Every bosom heaved with unfeigned emotions of sorrow and gratitude; and, if that moment were to be the last, every soul that were present, would be willing and sincere witnesses to the merits of the departed Hero. – Oh! immortal Nelson! if it were possible for thy spirit to hover over the place where thy remains are deposited, what bliss ecstatic must those not have enjoyed in the contemplation of the tribute of feeling and respect paid to thy memory by all descriptions of they fellow subjects.

The staves were then broken by the King at Arms, and the style, titles and dignities of the deceased Peer, were proclaimed, and the awful ceremonial closed by the colours of the Victory being deposited with the Chieftain who so gloriously fell under them!

The honest tars, however, who bore into the church the ensigns of the Victory, desirous of retaining some mementoes of their great and favourite commander, tore off a considerable part of the largest flag, of which most, if not all, of them obtained a small portion; though few other persons were able to get any of it.

The Speech of Sir Isaac Heard, Garter King at Arms, is announcing the style and titles of the deceased, had an impressive effect, from the very articulate and pathetic manner in which it was pronounced. The words were nearly as follows:

"Thus it has pleased Almighty God to take, out of this transitory life, unto his divine mercy, the most Noble Lord Horatio Nelson, Viscount and Baron Nelson of the Nile, and of Burnham Thorpe, in the County of Norfolk, Baron Nelson of the Nile, and of Hilborough in the same county; Knight of the most Honourable the Order of the Bath; Vice-admiral of the White Squadron of the Fleet, and commander in Chief of his Majesty's ships and vessels in the Mediterranean; also Duke of Bronte in Sicily; Knight Grand Cross of the Sicilian Order of St. Ferdinand and of Merit; Member of the Ottoman Order of the Crescent; Knight Grand Commander of the Order of St. Joachim; and the Hero who, in the moment of victory, fell covered with immortal glory. Let us humbly trust that he is now raised to bliss ineffable, and to a glorious immortality!"

SERVICES AND ANTHEMS

Sung as the Procession moved from the great West Door, by the Minor Canons, Vicars Choral, & etc. of St. Paul's Cathedral, assisted by the Priests and Gentlemen of his Majesty's Chapels Royal, and Minor Canons and Vicars Choral of the collegiate Church of St. Peter, Westminster, and others.

(The Music by Dr. Croft)

I am the Resurrection and the Life, saith the Lord: he that believeth in me, though he were dead, yet shall he live. And whosoever liveth and believeth in me, shall never die. *St. John* xi.25, 26.

I know that my Redeemer liveth, and that he shall stand at the later day upon the earth. And though after my skin, worms destroy this body; yet in my flesh shall I see God: whom I shall see for myself, and mine eyes shall behold, and not another. *Job.* xix. 25, 26, 27.

We brought nothing into this world, and it is certain we can carry nothing out. The Lord gave, and the Lord hath taken away; blessed be the name of the Lord. 1 *Tim.* vi. 7. *Job.* i. 21.

Then was sung, in the course of the Service, Dixi Custodiam, *Psalm* xxxix.

I said, I will take heed to my ways: that I offend not in my tongue.

I will keep my mouth as it were with a bridle: while the ungodly is in my sight.

I held my tongue, and spoke nothing: I kept silence, yea, even from good words; but it was pain and grief to me.

My heart was hot within me; and while I was thus musing, the fire kindled: and at the last I spake with my tongue.

Lord, let me know mine end, and the number of my days: that I may be certified how long I have to live.

Behold, thou hast made my days as it were a span long: and mine age is even as nothing in respect of thee; and verily every man living is altogether vanity.

For man walketh in a vain shadow, and disquieteth himself in vain: he heapeth up riches and cannot tell who shall gather them.

And now, Lord, what is my hope: truly my hope is even in thee.

Deliver me from all mine offences: and make me not a rebuke unto the foolish.

I became dumb, and opened not my mouth: for it was thy doing.

Take thy plague away from me: I am even consumed by means of they heavy hand.

When thou was rebukes dost chasten man for sin, though makest his beauty to consume away, like as it were a moth fretting a garment: every man therefore is but vanity.

Hear my prayer, O Lord, and with thine ears consider my calling; held not they peace at my tears.

For I am a stranger with thee: and a sojourner, as all my fathers were.

O spare me a little, that I may recover my strength: before I go hence, and be no more seen.

Glory be to the Father, and to the Son, and to the Holy Ghost;

As it was in the beginning, is now, and ever shall be; world without end. *Amen.*

Domine, refugium. Psalm xc.

Lord, thou hast been our refuge: from one generation to another.

Before the mountains were brought forth, or ever the earth and the world were made: thou art God from everlasting, and world without end.

Thou turnest man to destruction: again, thou sayest, Come again, ye children of men.

For a thousand years in thy sight are but as yesterday: seeing that is past as a watch in the night.

As soon as thou scatterest them, they are even as a sleep: and fade away suddenly like the grass.

In the morning it is green and groweth up; but in the evening it is cut down, dried up, and withered.

For we consume away in thy displeasure: and are afraid at they wrathful indignation.

Thou hast set our misdeeds before thee: and our secret sins in the light of thy countenance.

For when thou art angry, all our days are gone: we bring our years to an end, as it were a tale that is told.

The days of our age are threescore years and ten; and though men be so strong, that they come to fourscore years; yet is their strength then but labour and sorrow; so soon passeth it away, and we are gone.

But who regardeth the power of thy wrath: for even thereafter as a man feareth, so is they displeasure.

So teach us to number our days; that we may apply our hearts unto wisdom.

Turn thee again, O Lord, at the last; and be gracious unto thy servants.

O satisfy us with thy mercy, and that soon; so shall we rejoice and be glad all the days of our life.

Comfort us again, now after the time that thou hast plagued us: and for the years wherein we have suffered adversity.

Shew thy servants they work: and their children thy glory.

And the glorious Majesty of the Lord our God be upon us: prosper thou the work of our hands upon us, O prosper thou our handy work.

Glory be to the Father, and to the Son, and to the Holy Ghost;

As it was in the beginning, is now, and ever shall be; world without end. *Amen.*

Magnificat (or the Song of the blessed Virgin Mary).
St. Luke, i. 46.

My soul doth magnify the Lord; and my spirit hath rejoiced in God my Saviour.

For he hath regarded the lowliness of his hand-maiden.

For behold, from henceforth: all generations shall call me blessed.

For he that is mighty hath magnified me: and holy is his Name.

And his mercy is on them that fear him: throughout all generations.

He hath shewed strength with his arm: he hath scattered the proud in the imagination of their hearts.

He hath put down the mighty from their seat: and the rich he hath sent empty away.

He remembering his mercy, hath holpen his servant Israel: as he promised to our forefathers, Abraham and his seed for ever. Glory be to the Father, and to the Son, and to the Holy Ghost; As it was in the beginning, is now, and ever shall be: world without end. *Amen.*

Anthem. Psalm xxxix

CHORUS

5. Lord, let me know my end, and the number of my days: that I may be certified how long I have to live.

6. Thou hast made my days as it were a span long; and mine age is nothing in respect of Thee, and verily every man living is altogether vanity.

TREBLES

7. For man walketh in a vain shadow, and disquieteth himself in vain: he heapeth up riches, and cannot tell who shall gather them.

CHORUS

8. And now, Lord, what is my hope? truly my hope is even in Thee.

13. Hear my Prayer, O Lord, and with thine ear consider my calling: hold not thy peace at my tears.

15. O spare me a little, that I may recover my strength; before I go hence, and be no more seen.

After the Evening Service was ended, the Corpse was carried to the Place of Interment; during which Time a grand solemn Dirge was played on the Organ; after which was sung:

Man that is born of a woman, hath but a short time to live, and is full of misery. He cometh up, and is cut down like a flower; he fleeth as it were a shadow, and never continueth in one stay.

In the midst of life we are in death: of whom may we seek for succour, but of thee, O Lord, who for our sins art justly displeased?

Yet, O Lord God most holy, O Lord most mighty, O holy and most merciful Saviour, deliver us not into the bitter pains of eternal death.

Thou knowest, Lord, the secrets of our hearts: shut not thy merciful ears to our prayer; but spare us, Lord most holy, O God most mighty, O holy and merciful Saviour, thou most worthy judge eternal, suffer us not at our last hour, for any pains of death, to fall from thee.

Then the officiating Minister said:

Forasmuch as it hath pleased Almighty God, of his great mercy, to take unto himself the soul of our dear brother here departed, we therefore commit his body to the ground; earth to earth, ashes to ashes, dust to dust; in sure and certain hope of the resurrection to eternal life, through our Lord Jesus Christ, who shall change our vile body, that it may be like unto his glorious body, according to the mighty working, whereby he is able to subdue all things to himself.

After which was sung by the whole Choir:

I heard a voice from heaven saying unto me, Write, from henceforth blessed are the dead, which die in the Lord: even so saith the spirit; for they rest from their labours. *Rev.* xiv. 13.

Concluding Anthem

Verse. His body is buried in peace.

Chorus. But his name liveth evermore.

The interment was concluded a little before six, but the church was not cleared by nine o'clock. In the procession there were, according to the nearest calculation we were enabled to form of it as it passed us, of Gentlemen and Esquiries, about 200, of Members of the House of Commons, about 60, of Peers, about 40. The number of Naval Officers exceeded a hundred; the Military were about 50; and there were nearly an equal number of Clergymen.

The most interesting part of the cavalcade, that which was certainly best calculated to make a strange impression upon the minds of the spectators, was the exhibition made by a part of the crew of the Victory. Of that gallant body about 60 were in the church, and they bore two union jacks and the St. George's ensign belonging to the Victory. These colours were perforated in various places by the shot of the enemy. Several parts of the ensign were, in fact, literally shattered; these parts the seamen particularly exposed to view, and the effect of such an exhibition may be easily imagined. As soon, indeed, as the seamen and colours came in sight, they became the principal object of attention. This was naturally to be expected. That man's mind must be irregularly constructed, it must be insensible to merit, it must be unsusceptible of glory, it must be indifferent to patriotism, if motive do not ever occur to his thoughts of sufficient strength to induce him to look with peculiar reverence to such men, particularly under the circumstances of the occasion. Upon the countenances of these gallant fellows there was an eloquent expression of sorrow. Features which could never be taught or formed to express fear or unmanly feeling seemed to be considerably softened. These men, whom no dangers could daunt, whose nerves would stand unshaken before the most menacing terrors of death, seemed deeply depressed by the fate of their commander. Their affection was so apparent as to excite the most lively sympathy on the hearts of the spectators.

This funeral of a hero, who has achieved, in the service of his country, the greatest navel exploits that were ever performed by any conqueror that has yet exited, was attended by the seven sons of his Sovereign, by the chief nobility, gentry, and merchants of the empire, and by many thousands of subjects of all classes, with a universal, an unmixed, and a heart-felt sense of grief for his loss; but at the same time with a glorious exultation in the deeds by which his life has been adorned, and his death consecrated to immortal honours. We trust that while the name of Nelson is remembered, we shall never want those who are animated by his zeal, and are ardently desirous of imitating his brilliant example.

Report states, that the funeral will cost £30,000, independently of the monument.

The Funeral Car was on Friday placed in the middle of the King's Mews, and exhibited for the gratification of those who might not have had a view of it on the day of the grand national procession.